MY BODY Inside and Out!

My Amazing Sense of Smell

by Ruth Owen

Consultant:

Suzy Gazlay, MA
Recipient, Presidential Award for Excellence in Science Teaching

Published in 2014 by Ruby Tuesday Books Ltd.

Copyright © 2014 Ruby Tuesday Books Ltd.

All rights reserved. No part of this publication may be reproduced in whole or in part, stored in any retrieval system, or transmitted in any form or by any means, electronic, mechanical, photocopying, recording, or otherwise, without written permission from the publisher.

Editor: Mark J. Sachner
Designer: Emma Randall
Production: John Lingham

Photo credits:
Shutterstock: Cover, 1, 4–5, 6–7, 8–9, 10–11, 12–13, 14–15, 16–17, 18–19, 20, 21 (top), 23; Superstock: 21 (bottom).

Library of Congress Control Number: 2013919033

ISBN 978-1-909673-36-6

Printed and published in the United States of America

For further information including rights and permissions requests, please contact our Customer Service Department at 877-337-8577.

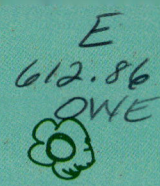

E
612.86
OWE

Contents

Smells All Around 4
What Is a Smell? 6
Get to Know Your Nose 8
Capturing Smells 10
Smelly Messages 12
Putting It All Together 14
Smelling and Tasting 16
Your Nose Fights Back! 18
Care For Your Sense of Smell 20

Glossary 22
Index 24
Read More 24
Learn More Online 24

Words shown in **bold** in the text are
explained in the glossary.

Smells All Around

Yuck. Stinky. Whose sneakers are those?

Mmmmm. Yummy. How soon can I eat one of those freshly baked cookies?

Every day, your **sense** of smell brings you hundreds of different smells.

Some smells, like the perfume of a flower, make your world a nicer place to be.

Others, like the smell of smoke, can sometimes help warn you of danger.

What exactly are smells, though, and how are you able to smell them?

Your body has five senses, which are seeing, hearing, smelling, tasting, and touching. Your senses help you enjoy your world and help keep you safe.

What Is a Smell?

You can't see a smell with your eyes, so what is it actually made of?

Everything around you, including your own body, is made of tiny parts called **atoms**.

When two or more atoms join together, they make a **molecule**.

Every smell that your nose detects is made of molecules.

When you cut open an orange, tiny molecules of fruity **liquid** float into the air.

The molecules are much too tiny to see, but when they float into your nose, you smell the orange.

Molecules of orange smell

Some smell molecules are made of **gas**. Others are made of liquid. Some smell molecules are actually tiny solid pieces of an object.

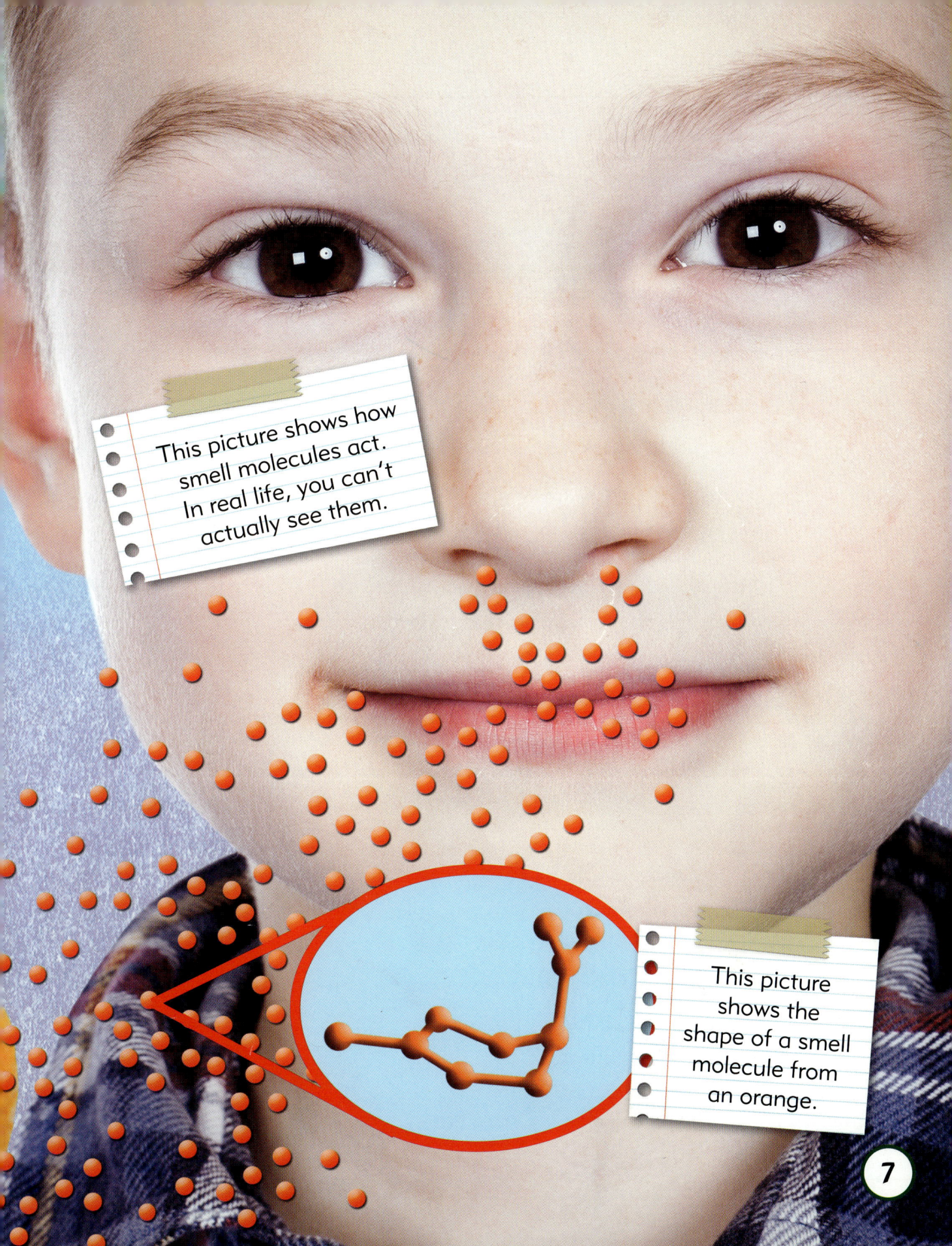

This picture shows how smell molecules act. In real life, you can't actually see them.

This picture shows the shape of a smell molecule from an orange.

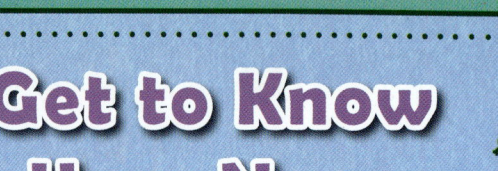

Get to Know Your Nose

It's your nose's job to capture the smell molecules floating in the air around you.

When you breathe in, air and smell molecules are sucked into your nostrils.

Each nostril leads to a short tunnel called a **nasal passage**.

Each passage leads to an open space inside your head called a **nasal cavity**.

From your nostrils, air and smells travel along your nasal passages into your nasal cavity.

Your nostrils, nasal passages, and nasal cavity are separated by a thin wall called the septum. Your septum is made of tough, rubbery **tissue** called **cartilage**.

Nostril

Septum

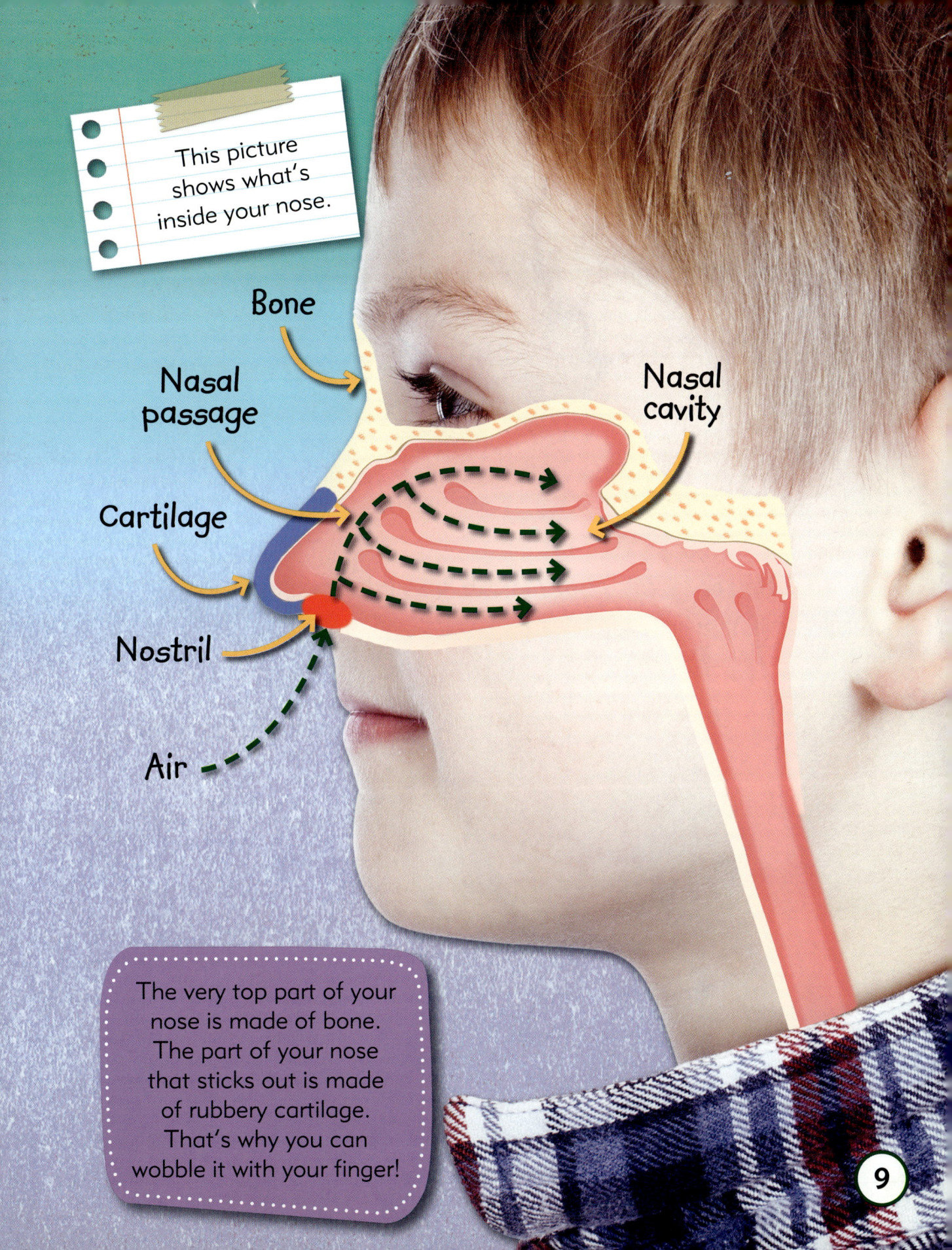

Capturing Smells

Once smell molecules are in your nasal cavity, the inside parts of your nose get to work.

At the top of your nasal cavity, there is an area that traps smell molecules.

This area is packed with millions of tiny parts called **receptors**.

The receptors capture the smell molecules that enter your nose.

Smell molecules

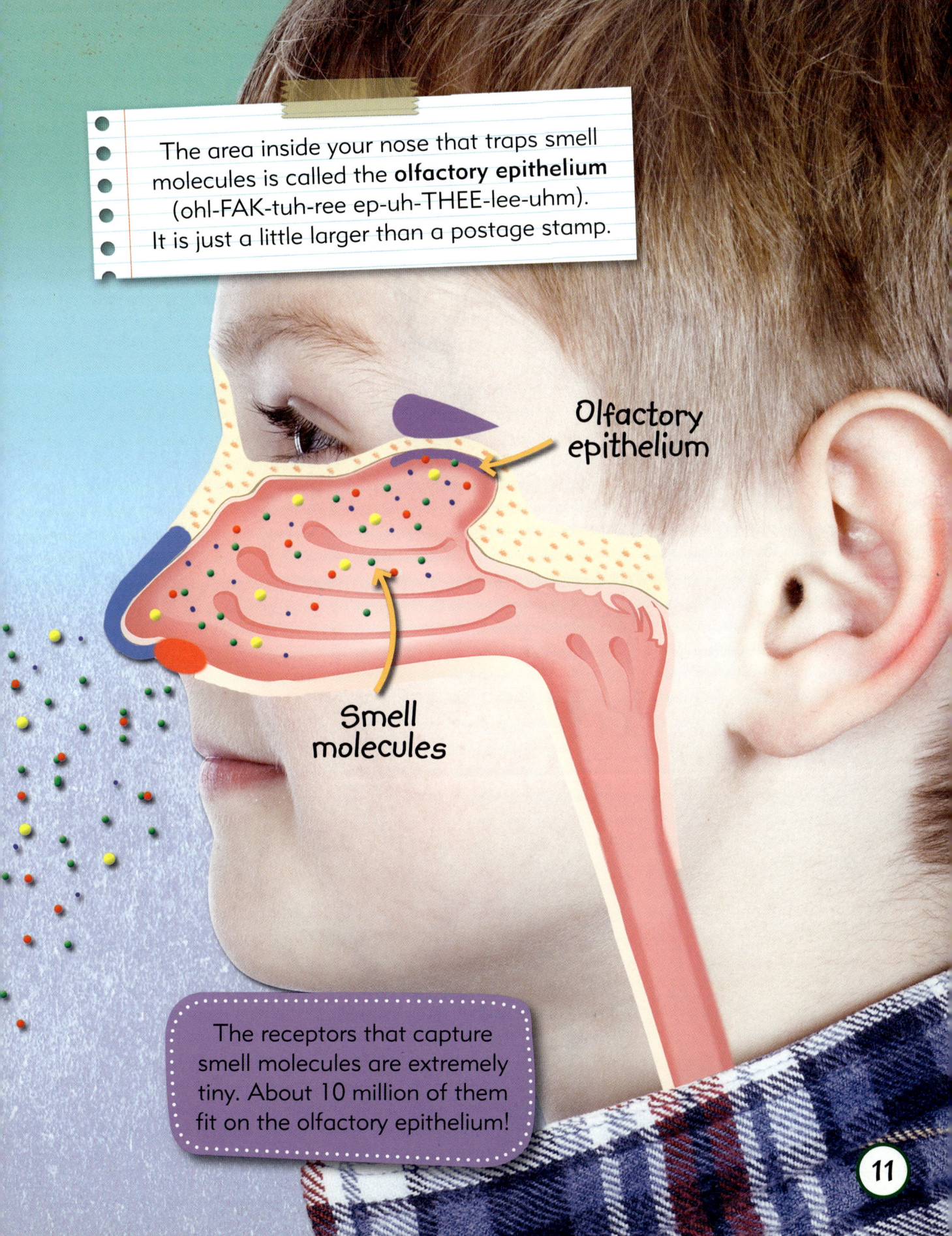

Smelly Messages

The millions of receptors inside your nose are busy capturing smell molecules day and night.

Once a receptor captures a molecule, it sends a message to your **olfactory bulb**.

Then your olfactory bulb passes the message on to your brain.

To get to your brain, the message speeds along a pathway of **cells** called **nerve cells**.

The message gives your brain lots of information about the smell molecule.

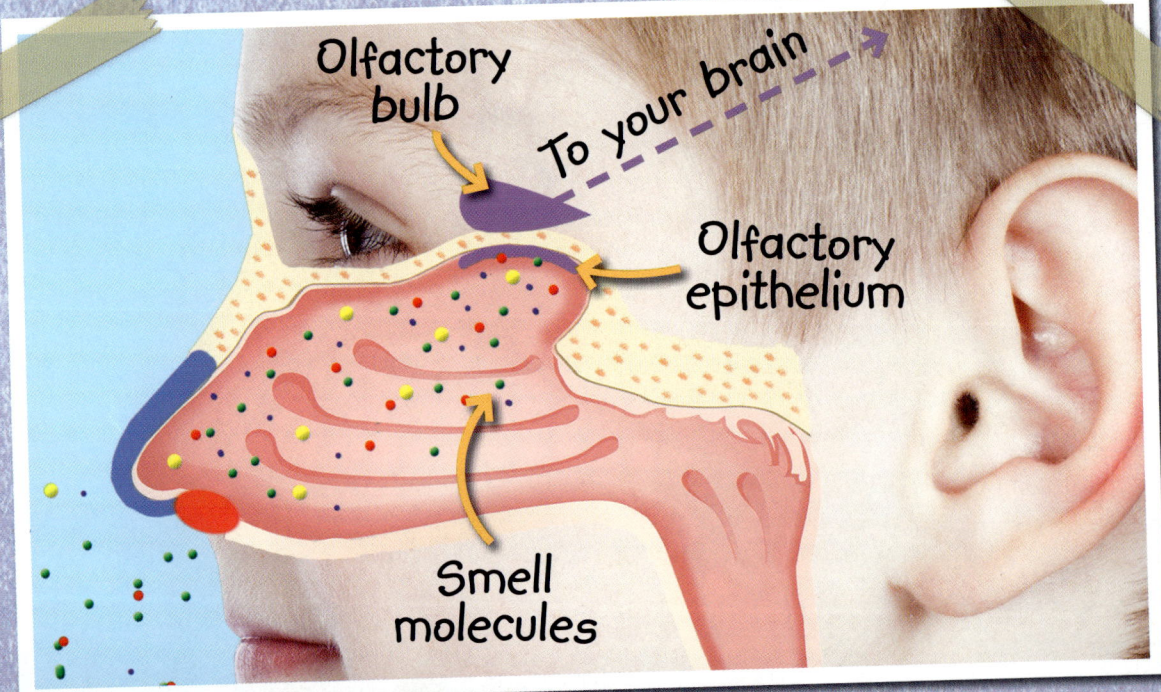

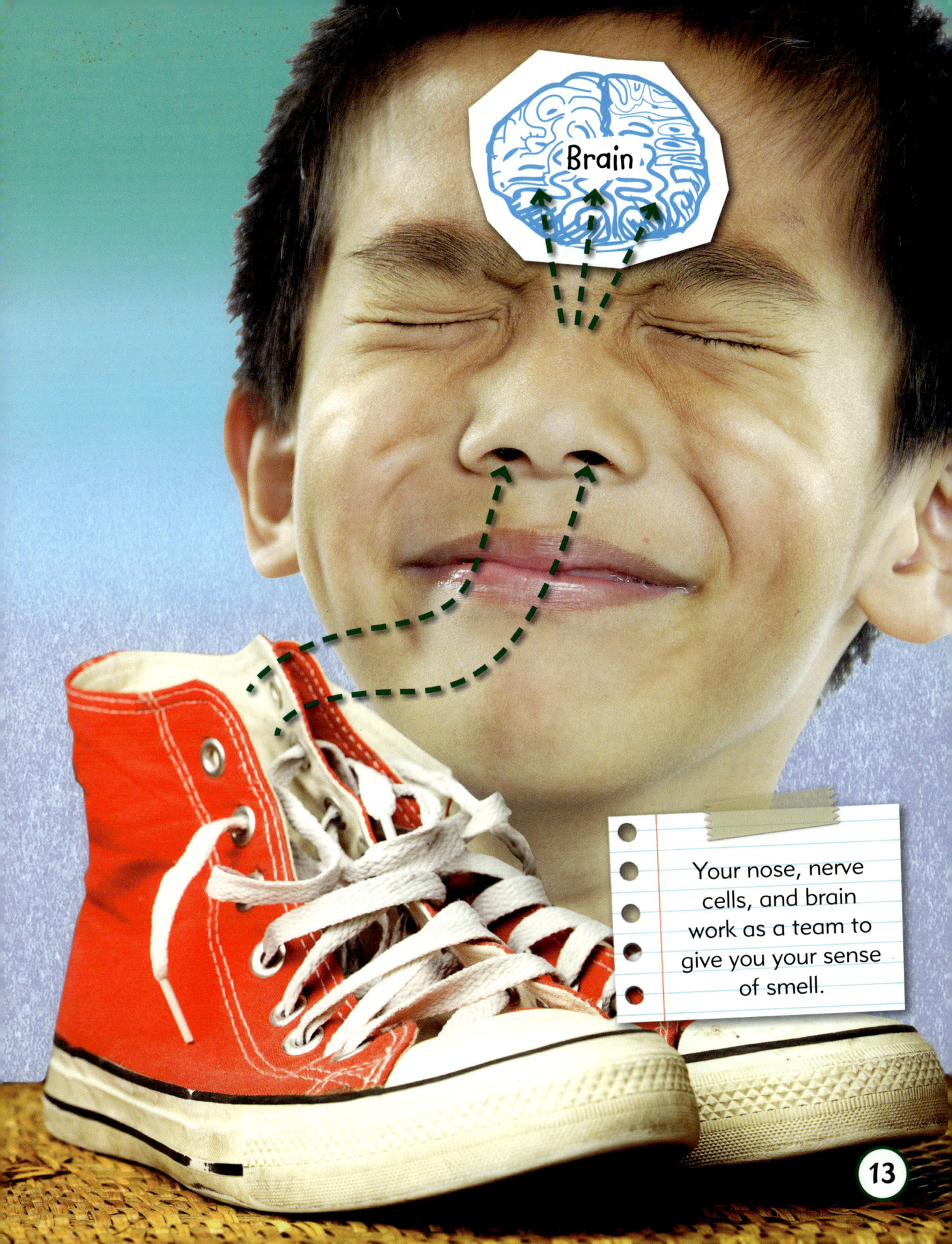

Brain

Your nose, nerve cells, and brain work as a team to give you your sense of smell.

13

Putting It All Together

When messages from your nose reach your brain, it instantly goes into action.

Your brain figures out what the smell is, and then you smell oranges, pizza, or stinky sneakers.

Your brain remembers and can recognize thousands of different smells.

Recognizing smells can help keep you safe.

For example, when your nose breathes in smoke, your brain recognizes the smell.

Your brain tells you the smell is smoke so you know there could be a fire nearby.

Your brain can recognize about 10,000 different smells!

Your sense of smell protects you from eating or drinking something that could make you sick. For example, when milk has gone bad, your nose and brain work together to bring you the horrible sour smell. Then you know not to drink the milk.

Smelling and Tasting

When you eat or drink, your nose teams up with your tongue to taste what's in your mouth.

Before you begin eating, your nose breathes in smell molecules from your food.

Once you are chewing your food, smell molecules travel from your mouth up into your nose.

At the same time, tiny **taste buds** on your tongue detect the flavors in your food.

Your nose and taste buds send messages to your brain about the food.

Your brain uses this information to tell you how the food tastes.

Your tongue contains about 10,000 taste buds. They are so small, they can only be seen with a **microscope**.

Have you ever noticed that sometimes when you have a cold, you can't taste your food? Your taste buds are still working. Your blocked nose can't smell the food, though, so you can't taste it properly.

Try holding your nose next time you eat. Without your sense of smell, it will be difficult to taste the full flavor of your food.

Your Nose Fights Back!

Day and night, your nose is helping you breathe in and out.

The air you breathe in through your nose goes down into your lungs.

Sometimes the air you breathe contains tiny pieces of dirt or **germs** that can harm your lungs.

To stop these invaders from getting into your body, your nose produces a sticky substance called **mucus**.

When dirt or germs are breathed in by your nose, they get trapped in the mucus.

You probably call the mucus in your nose by another name—snot! Every day you produce about 2 pints (1 liter) of this helpful mucus.

Sometimes something, such as dust, gets stuck up your nose. Then your nose starts to itch and tickle.

Your nose sends a message to the sneeze center in your brain. The message says, "Get these invaders out, now!"

Your brain tells muscles in your belly, chest, throat, and face to work together to make a sneeze.

A-CHOO!
The invaders are blasted from your nose at high speed!

Care For Your Sense of Smell

Each day, your nose breathes in air thousands of times.

Every breath of air contains smell molecules.

Some smells tell you there's a problem, such as burning toast!

Others make you feel good, such as the smell of fresh sheets on your bed.

Your amazing sense of smell helps tell you all about the world around you.

So take good care of your nose, and keep on sniffing!

Never poke anything up your nose, not even your finger! You could hurt your nasal passages and put germs into your nose.

When you sneeze, cover your nose and mouth with a tissue. Or you can sneeze into the inside of your elbow. Remember, you're blasting germs and other unwanted stuff out of your nose. So you don't want to blast it all over someone else!

If you want to have a good sense of smell, don't ever smoke. Smoking can damage a person's sense of smell.

Glossary

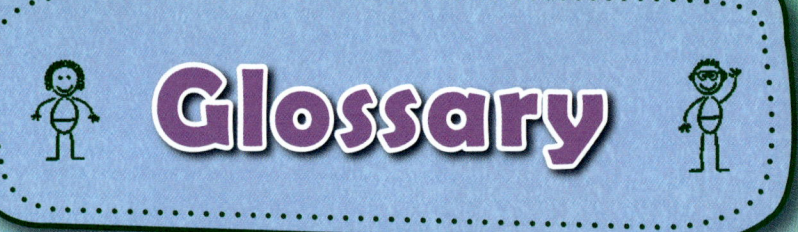

atoms (AT-uhmz)
Pieces of matter that are the building blocks of everything around you. For example, this book is made of atoms. Even you are made of trillions of atoms. Atoms can only be seen with very powerful types of microscopes.

cartilage (KAR-tuh-lij)
Strong, rubbery tissue found in many areas of the body, including your nose and ears.

cells (SELZ)
Very tiny parts of a living thing. Your bones, muscles, skin, hair, and every part of you are made of cells. Cells are tiny, but not as tiny as atoms or molecules.

gas (GASS)
A substance, such as oxygen or helium, that floats in the air. A gas does not have a definite shape or size.

germ (JUHRM)
A tiny living thing that is too small for you to see. Germs can harm your body or make you sick.

liquid (LIK-wid)
A substance, such as water, that is not solid and not a gas. A liquid flows and changes its shape to fit any container it is poured into.

microscope (MIKE-ruh-skope)
A tool or very powerful machine that is used to see things that are too small for a person to see with his or her eyes alone.

molecule (MAHL-uh-kyool)
A group of two or more atoms that are joined together.

mucus (MYOO-kuhss)
A sticky substance that your body produces to help protect itself.

nasal cavity (NAY-zuhl CAV-uh-tee)
A space inside your head. When you breathe in air through your nostrils, it goes along your nasal passages into your nasal cavity.

nasal passage (NAY-zuhl PASS-ij)
A short tunnel in your nose that leads from your nostril to your nasal cavity.

nerve cell (NURV SEL)
One of the billions of tiny cells that carry information between your brain and other parts of your body.

olfactory bulb
(ohl-FAK-tuh-ree BUHLB)
A tiny body part that is positioned in your head and sends information about smell from your nose to your brain.

olfactory epithelium
(ohl-FAK-tuh-ree ep-uh-THEE-lee-uhm)
A small area of tissue at the top of your nasal cavity. It contains millions of tiny receptors that capture smell molecules.

receptor (rih-SEP-tuhr)
One of millions of tiny parts in your nose that capture smell molecules.

sense (SENSS)
One of the five ways that you collect information about the world around you. Your senses are seeing, hearing, smelling, tasting, and touching.

taste bud (TAYST BUHD)
A microscopic group of cells on your tongue that detect the flavors in your food. Your taste buds send information about the flavors to your brain so that you can taste your food.

tissue (TISH-yoo)
A group of connected cells in your body that work together. Cells are very tiny parts of a living thing. Skin tissue, for example, is made up of skin cells.

Index

A
air 6, 8–9, 20
atoms 6

B
bone 9
brain 12–13, 14–15, 16, 19
breathing 8, 14, 16, 18, 20

C
cartilage 8–9
cells 12
colds 17

F
flavors 16–17

G
gases 6
germs 18, 20–21

L
lungs 18

M
microscopes 16
molecules 6–7, 8, 10–11, 12, 16, 20
mouth 16, 21
mucus 18
muscles 19

N
nasal cavity 8–9, 10
nasal passages 8–9, 20
nerve cells 12–13
nose 6, 8–9, 10, 12–13, 14–15, 16–17, 18–19, 20–21
nostrils 8–9

O
olfactory bulb 12
olfactory epithelium 11, 12

R
receptors 10–11, 12

S
senses 4, 13, 15, 17, 20–21
septum 8
smells 4, 6–7, 8, 10–11, 12, 14–15, 16, 20
smoking 21
sneeze center 19
sneezing 19, 21
snot 18

T
taste buds 16–17
tasting 4, 16–17
tongue 16

Read More

Olien, Rebecca. *Smelling (First Facts)*. North Mankato, MN: Capstone Press (2006).

Weiss, Ellen. *The Sense of Smell (New True Books)*. Danbury, CT: Children's Press (2009).

Learn More Online

To learn more about your sense of smell, go to
www.rubytuesdaybooks.com/mybodysmell